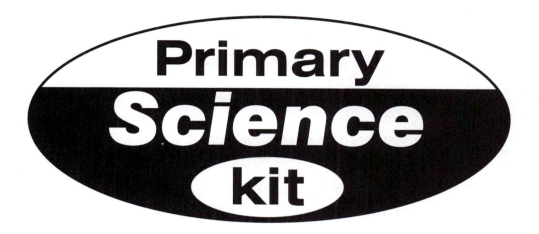

Primary Science kit

Pupil Resource Book
Years 1–2

Rosemary Sherrington

Published in 2002 by:
Nelson Thornes Ltd
Delta Place
27 Bath Road
CHELTENHAM
GL53 7TH
United Kingdom

04 05 06 / 10 9 8 7 6 5

A catalogue record for this book is available from the British Library

ISBN 0 7487 6484 4

Illustrations by Sarah Geeves, Sascha Lipscomb, Juliette Nicolson, Philip Orchard, Clyde Pearson and David Woodroffe

Cover photographs © Digital Stock (NT)

Page make-up by AMR Ltd

Printed in Great Britain by Antony Rowe

Contents

PAS1 / **Our bodies**

Name .... Date ....

Draw lines to join each part of the body to its name.

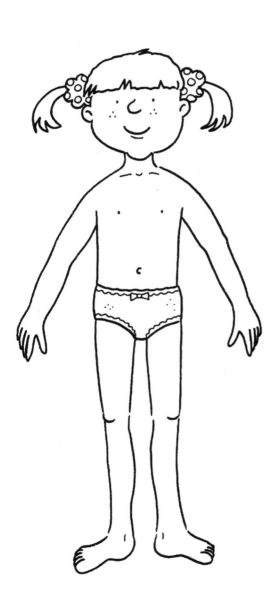

head

face

neck

shoulder

chest

arm

hand

leg

foot

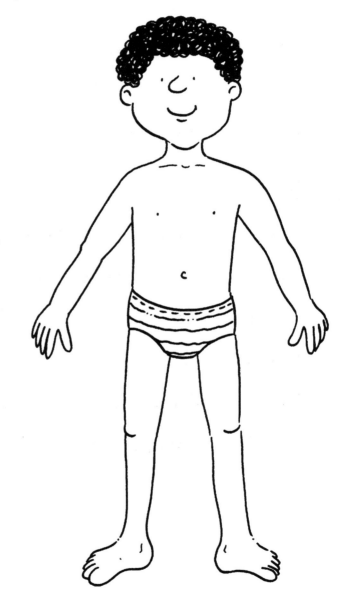

Think of some other parts.

Write their names here: _____ _____

My face

Name .... **Date** ....

Draw a big picture of your face.

Write these names in the correct places on your drawing.

head	ear	forehead	cheek
eye	mouth	eyelashes	lip
nose	chin	eyebrow	

Our sense organs

Name .... **Date** ....

Finish the picture.
Draw lines to join the labels to the right places.

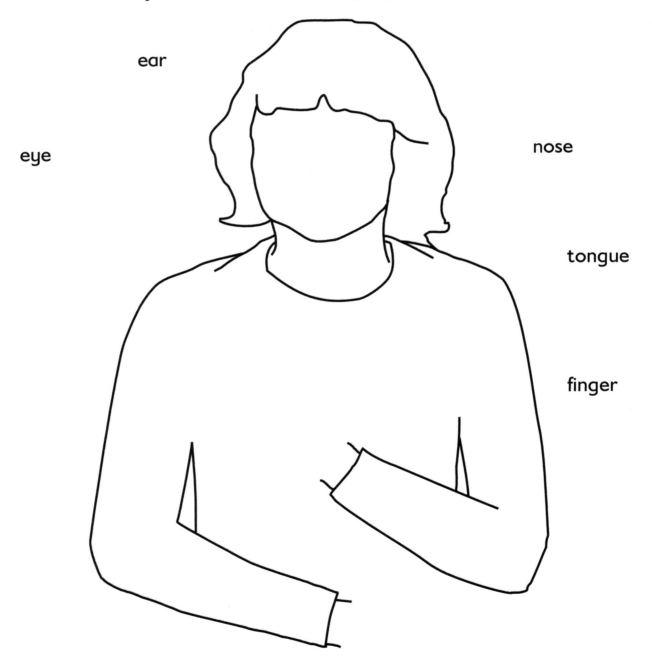

ear

eye

nose

tongue

finger

YEAR 1 **1.1.4**

PAS4 # A baby

Name .... **Date** ....

I can

I cannot

How we move

Name .... Date ....

Growing older

Name .... **Date** ....

Match the animals with their young.

Hair colours

Name .... **Date** ....

Put a ✓ for every person in your group.

black

_____

brown

_____

blond

_____

auburn

_____

fair

_____

Food we eat

Name .... **Date** ....

What do you eat or drink?

cheese

carrots

potatoes

tomato

cereal

bread

crisps

fizzy drinks

dinner

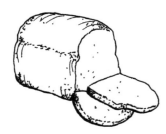

biscuits

fruit tart

cake

cakes

Unit 1 Ourselves

Name .... **Date** ....

Draw lines to join the words to the parts of the body correctly.

shoulder

elbow

wrist

hip

knuckles

knee

ankle

head

body

arm

leg

hand

foot

Is he an animal? _____

Let's grow plants

Name .... **Date** ....

This is how our seeds grew.

Name of seed _____

Date _____

Date _____

Date _____

Name the parts of the plant.

PAS11 **Plants we eat**

Name .... **Date** ....

Draw the part we eat.
What part of the plant is it?

carrot

_____

broccoli

_____

lettuce

_____

celery

_____

cauliflower

_____

parsnip

_____

Name .... **Date** ....

Roots look like this.

Water and light

Name .... **Date** ....

Tick (✓) yes or no.

Do plants need water to grow?

yes ☐   no ☐

Draw your seeds.

Do plants need light to grow?

yes ☐   no ☐

Draw your seeds.

PAS14 Animals and plants are alive

Name .... **Date** ....

What do animals and plants do?

animals   plants

☐ feed ☐

☐ grow ☐

☐ have babies ☐

☐ sense things ☐

Tick (✓) the things animals do.

Tick (✓) the things plants do.

Unit 2 Growing plants

Name .... **Date** ....

1 Tick (✓) what plants need to grow well.

water ☐

chips ☐

biscuit ☐

light ☐

2 Tick (✓) plants we eat.

tree ☐   broccoli ☐   carrot ☐   daisies ☐

3 Do these both grow? _____

feed? _____

have babies? _____

Are they both alive? _____

Primary Science Kit: Pupil Resource Book Years 1–2 © Rosemary Sherrington, Nelson Thornes Ltd, 2002

PAS16 A material hunt

Name .... **Date** ....

I found materials that are made of _____ .

Draw and name what you found.

PAS17 **Things made of wood**

Name .... **Date** ....

Draw and describe things made of wood.

What are things made of?

Name .... Date ....

wood   clay   wool

metal   glass   paper

plastic   rubber   cotton

Draw lines to join the objects to the name of the material
they are made from.

Primary Science Kit: Pupil Resource Book Years 1–2 © Rosemary Sherrington, Nelson Thornes Ltd, 2002

PAS19 The best material

Name .... **Date** ....

Find the best material for a doll's house window and a toy slide.

Draw a doll's house.

Stick the material
for the window here.

Words _____

Draw a toy slide.

Stick the material
for the slide here.

Words _____

Magnets attract some things

Name .... **Date** ....

A magnet attracts these.	A magnet does not attract these.

These objects are all made of _____ .

YEAR 1 1.3.6

PAS21 **Is it waterproof?**

Name .... Date ....

Material	Waterproof	Not waterproof

Unit 3 Materials

Name .... **Date** ....

1 What are these? What are they made from?

_____   _____   _____

_____   _____   _____

_____   _____   _____

_____   _____   _____

2 Which would be best for a window?

jelly   wood   glass   plastic   paper   _____

3 Tick which are attracted to a magnet.

paper clip    steel scissors   eraser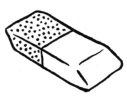

Primary Science Kit: Pupil Resource Book Years 1–2 © Rosemary Sherrington, Nelson Thornes Ltd, 2002

PAS23 Darkness

Name .... **Date** ....

Draw some places where it is dark inside.

I can *see* in the dark with a _____ .

I can find things in the dark with my _____ .

Tick the right word.

When it is really dark I can/I cannot *see*.

Sources of light

Name .... **Date** ....

Draw some sources of light. Write their names.

Draw an arrow to show where the light comes from. Write the name.

Unit 4 Light and dark

Name .... Date ....

1 Draw two sources of light.

2 Can we see in the dark?   _____

3 Write the name of a shiny object.   _____

4 Does the object shine in darkness?   _____

5 What does it need to make it shine? _____

6 Why is it dangerous to look at the sun?

_____

Primary Science Kit: Pupil Resource Book Years 1–2 © Rosemary Sherrington, Nelson Thornes Ltd, 2002

Animals moving

Name .... Date ....

Wordcheck

Name .... Date ....

Ways animals move

leap	jump	pull
butt	push	hold
reach up	bite	gnaw
fly	swim	run

Add some more words.

_____

_____

_____

_____

_____

_____

Push or pull?

Name .... **Date** ....

Write push or pull.

Make the buggy move

Name .... **Date** ....

I can make it move by

_____

_____

_____

Primary Science Kit: Pupil Resource Book Years 1–2 © Rosemary Sherrington, Nelson Thornes Ltd, 2002

The force of wind

Name .... Date ....

Write what each one does in the wind.

PAS31 # Things that turn

Name .... **Date** ....

Name and colour the parts that turn.

_____

_____

_____

_____

_____

_____

Unit 5 Pushes and pulls

Name .... **Date** ....

1 How can you make the toy car move?

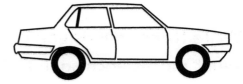

Give it a _____ or a _____ or a _____ .

2 Draw a safe place to cross a road.

3 Draw something that is moving because of the wind.

Ssh! What can you hear?

Name .... **Date** ....

Write three sounds you can hear in these places.
What makes each sound? Draw it.

In class	In the garden
On the street	**At the seaside**

Making sounds

Name .... Date ....

How do you make a sound with these?

Think of some more. Draw them. Write how they make sounds.

Musical instruments

Name .... **Date** ....

Draw the instruments.

Shake

Pluck

Bang

Blow

YEAR 1 1.6.4

PAS36

We hear with our ears

Name .... **Date** ....

Draw some things you can hear.

How well can you hear
with ear muffs on?

Draw a picture.

Write about what happened.

_____

_____

How far sound travels

Name .... **Date** ....

Our test

How far did the loud sound travel? _____

How far did the quiet sound travel? _____

Which one travelled the furthest? _____

Loud sounds	Quiet sounds

Unit 6 Sound and hearing

Name .... **Date** ....

1 Imagine you are going for a walk.
Draw things making sounds.

Quiet sounds   Loud sounds

Write the names of sounds.

Sounds I like   Sounds I don't like

_____   _____

_____   _____

_____   _____

_____   _____

2 Draw lines to join the instrument and how we play it.

pluck   tap

shake

bang   blow

Thinking about food

Name .... **Date** ....

This is what Lily is eating for her tea.

spaghetti   _____

meat sauce   _____

salad   _____

fruit   _____

custard   _____

a drink of water   _____

Write the names of the food groups these foods belong to.

PAS40 Grouping foods

Name .... **Date** ....

Write the names of the food groups.
Draw some foods for each group.

_____   _____

_____   _____

Our favourite foods

Name .... **Date** ....

Food	Number of children 👤 👤	Total

Food for a special occasion

Name .... **Date** ....

These are my favourite choices for a _____ .

Draw and write about your ideas.

We need exercise

Name .... **Date** ....

Draw yourself playing a game or doing PE.

Before the exercise I felt

After the exercise I felt

_____

_____

_____

_____

_____

_____

_____

_____

Using medicines safely

Name .... **Date** ....

Stick the sweet package here.   Stick the medicine package here.

I know which one is the medicine package because

_____

_____

_____

_____

Primary Science Kit: Pupil Resource Book Years 1–2 © Rosemary Sherrington, Nelson Thornes Ltd, 2002

Unit 1 Food, health, growth

Name .... **Date** ....

1 Draw or write the foods in each group.

Fruit and vegetables	Basic foods	Cheese or meat

2 Why do we need to eat and drink? _____

_____

3 These humans are growing. Write the name for each one.

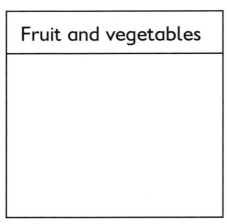 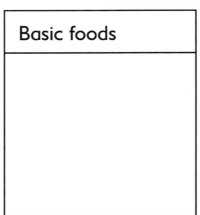 

_____   _____   _____

4 Write what you know about medicines.

_____

_____

PAS46 # Local wildlife

Name .... **Date** ....

We went to the _____ _____ to find plants and animals.

We found out where they live.

Animal or plant (draw)	Where I found it (write)

Plants and animals I know

Name .... **Date** ....

Draw three in each box. Write their names.

Birds

Flowers

Insects

Furry animals

Naming animals

Name .... **Date** ....

Find out the names of these animals.
Write about them.

_____

_____

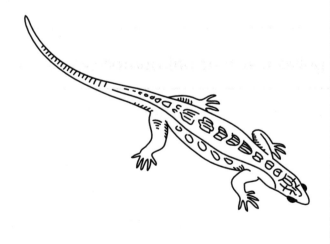

_____

_____

Different habitats

Name .... **Date** ....

Habitat (write)	Animals and plants found there (draw)

Did you find the animals and plants you expected?   yes ☐   no ☐

The two habitats are the same because _____

_____

They are different because _____

_____

Primary Science Kit: Pupil Resource Book Years 1–2 © Rosemary Sherrington, Nelson Thornes Ltd, 2002

Do seeds need water?

Name .... **Date** ....

We think *seeds need water to make them start to grow.*

We put _____ pea seeds in dry _____ and watered them.

We put _____ more in dry _____ and did not water them.

Water	No water

The seeds looked like this.

After _____ days
they looked like this.

After _____

After _____

Label the root and the shoot in your drawings.

Do seeds need water to germinate? _____

Were you right? _____

Primary Science Kit: Pupil Resource Book Years 1–2 © Rosemary Sherrington, Nelson Thornes Ltd, 2002

Do seeds need soil?

Name .... **Date** ....

We think only soil/compost will make seeds start to grow.

We put _____ pea seeds in compost.

We put _____ pea seeds in _____ .

We _____ _____ _____ _____ _____ _____ .

We watered them all.

Compost	_____	_____

The seeds looked like this.

After _____ days
they looked like this.

After _____ _____
they looked like this.

Do seeds need compost to germinate? _____

Will they grow   in _____?   _____

                        in _____?   _____

Were you right? _____

Label the
root and the
shoot in your
drawings.

Animal life cycles – frog

Name .... **Date** ....

A frog

Draw and label the stages in the life cycle of a frog.

Fill in the spaces.

_____ hatch from _____ .

Tadpoles grow _____ and change into tiny _____ .

Frogs lay _____ .

Animal life cycles – bird

Name .... **Date** ....

A bird

Draw and label the stages in the life cycle of a bird.

Fill in the spaces.

_____ hatch from _____ .

Chicks grow into _____ .

Birds lay _____ .

Animal life cycles – butterfly

A butterfly

Draw and label the stages in the life cycle of a butterfly.

Fill in the spaces.

_____ hatch from _____ .

Caterpillars grow, then become _____ .

From a pupa comes a _____ .

Butterflies lay _____ .

Unit 2 Plants and animals

Name .... **Date** ....

Write about a habitat you know.

The habitat is _____ .

These are some animals that live there.
(Draw them and write their names.)

These are some plants that live there.
(Draw them and write their names.)

These animals and plants live there because _____

_____

_____

A plant or an animal?

Name .... Date ....

Tick (✓) the animals.   Cross (✗) the plants.

I know an earthworm is _____ because _____ .

_____ .

I know a horse chestnut is _____ because

_____ .

I know a _____ is _____ because

_____ .

Are you a plant? _____

Are you an animal? _____

PAS57 # Animals

Name .... **Date** ....

Think of two answers to each question.

How are these animals like each other?

1 _____

2 _____

How do we know humans from other animals?

1 _____

2 _____

In what ways are humans like each other?

1 _____

2 _____

The same or different?

Name .... **Date** ....

Draw your friend.   Draw yourself.

Differences

_____   _____

_____   _____

_____   _____

Similarities

_____   _____

_____   _____

_____   _____

Primary Science Kit: Pupil Resource Book Years 1–2 © Rosemary Sherrington, Nelson Thornes Ltd, 2002

Who is it?

Name .... **Date** ....

Describe a member of the class so that other children can say who it is.

Who is it?

How many children were right? How many were wrong?
Make a tally.

	Total
Right	
Wrong	

More about plants

Name .... **Date** ....

Draw two different plants. Name them. Name the parts.

_____

_____

Write about differences between them.

_____

_____

_____

_____

How long are our hands?

Name .... **Date** ....

Measure your hands. Measure your friends' hands. Count in centimetres. Colour the squares.

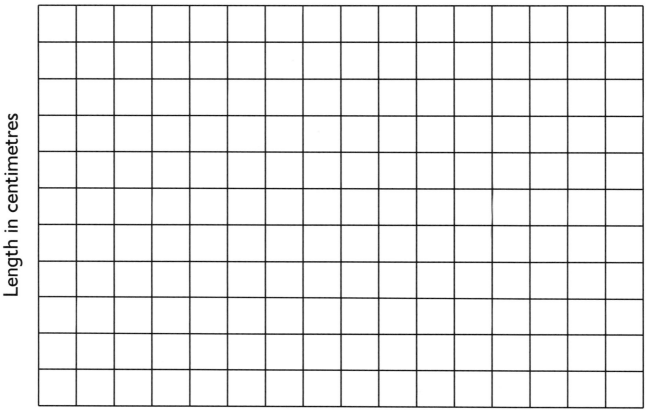

Length in centimetres

Me

Names

Whose is the longest? _____

Whose is the shortest? _____

Whose are the same? _____

Do hand sizes vary? _____

Unit 3 Variation

Name .... **Date** ....

Think about your friend and yourself.

1 Write three ways you are the same.

1 _____

2 _____

3 _____

2 Write three ways you are different.

1 _____

2 _____

3 _____

3 Write three ways you are both different from a plant.

1 _____

2 _____

3 _____

4 Draw a plant and label the

leaf   stem   root   flower

┌─────────────────────────────────┐
│ Draw on the back of the sheet. │
└─────────────────────────────────┘

Primary Science Kit: Pupil Resource Book Years 1–2 © Rosemary Sherrington, Nelson Thornes Ltd, 2002

Natural or made materials

Name .... **Date** ....

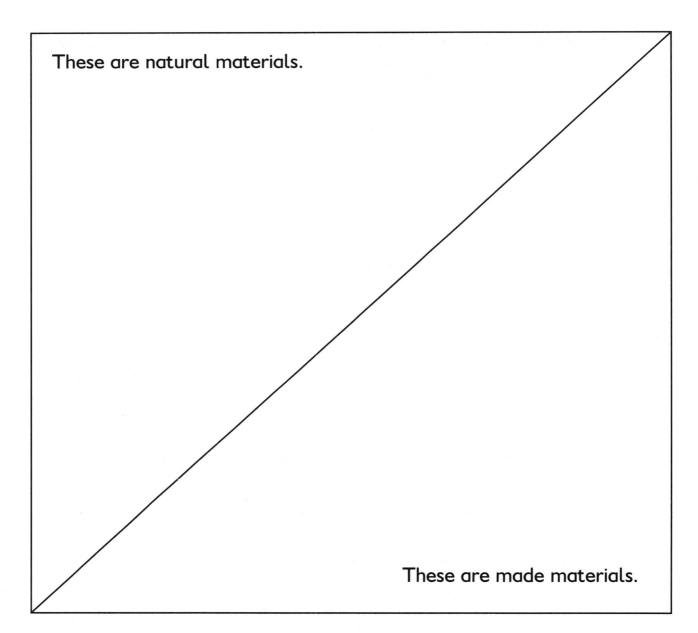

These are natural materials.

These are made materials.

Write the names of these materials in the correct set.

bone	paper	water
sand	clay	glass
plastic	grass	wood

Twist, stretch, bend, squash

Name .... **Date** ....

Draw and write ✓ or ✗.

Material	twist	stretch	bend	squash

These change back easily.	I cannot twist, stretch, bend or squash these.

The warmest place in class

Name .... **Date** ....

Fill in the table. Write what happened.

Time	Where we put the ice	What happened

Which ice cube melted the fastest? _____

Which ice cube melted the slowest? _____

Which is the warmest place in the classroom? _____

Unit 4 About materials

Name .... Date ....

Concept maps about materials

ice   steam   cool

change

heat

water

freeze

How can you join these words?

shiny   polyester

natural

made   rock

metal   natural   soft

plastic

wool   hard   wood

Pushes and pulls

Name .... **Date** ....

Objects I can move.	I moved it with a push pull

I can change the shape of these objects.
(Draw them and write their names.)

PAS68 # Speed up and slow down

Name .... **Date** ....

Draw a picture of yourself moving
fast on the apparatus.
Write about how you slow
yourself down.

This is how I slow myself down.

_____

_____

_____

_____

_____

Which car rolls furthest?

Name .... **Date** ....

I've rolled cars down a ramp to see which one rolled the furthest.
These are my results.

Car	How far it rolled		Longer distance
	1st time	2nd time	
1			
2			
3			

Which car went furthest? _____

Which car went the shortest distance? _____

Unit 5 Forces and movement

Name .... Date ....

1 Name some objects you can move with

a push   a pull

_____   _____

_____   _____

_____   _____

_____   _____

2 What can pushes or pulls make a toy or car do?

_____ _____ _____ _____

3 Some other children found out which car is the best roller.

This is their bar chart.

In their bar chart which
car travelled the furthest? _____

Which car went the
shortest distance? _____

Which cars went the
same distance? _____

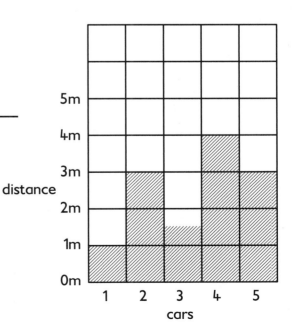

distance

PAS71 Things that use electricity

Name .... **Date** ....

I found things that use electricity to make them work.

I found out what they did and put them into sets.

YEAR 2 2.6.3

PAS72 # Using batteries

Name .... **Date** ....

Draw something that uses batteries. Name it.
Say what it does. Label the battery.

Write about how batteries can be dangerous.

_____

_____

_____

_____

Making things work

Name .... **Date** ....

Draw your circuit. Label the battery, the bulb, and the leads.

This is my electrical circuit.

It works because _____

_____

_____

_____

More circuits

Name .... **Date** ....

We looked at a circuit. It will not work because

_____ .

We tested our idea like this.

Did it work? _____

Our prediction was _____ .

It works now because _____ .

Make a switch

Name .... **Date** ....

Use a paper clip

   two paper fasteners

   a piece of card

5 cm

5 cm

Put the paper clip on the card and draw round it.

Make a hole at each end of the outline of the paper clip.

Push one paper fastener through each hole.

Attach the paper clip to one paper fastener.

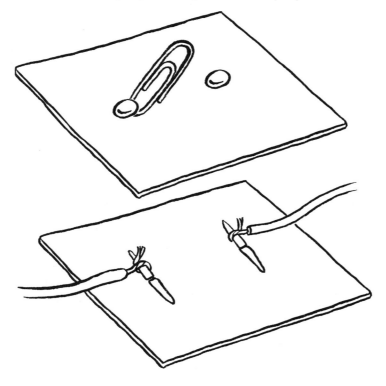

Fasten the wires onto the paper fasteners underneath the switch.

Primary Science Kit: Pupil Resource Book Years 1–2 © Rosemary Sherrington, Nelson Thornes Ltd, 2002

Use a switch

Name .... **Date** ....

Draw the circuit you made.

How does the switch work?

_____

_____

_____

Unit 6 Using electricity

615185

Name .... Date ....

1   Here is an electrical circuit.

Name the parts.

battery   wires
bulb and holder

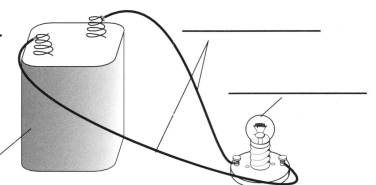

_____

_____

_____

2   Fill in the missing word.

A circuit must be _____ for electricity to flow.

3   Tick the circuit if it is complete and the bulb will light.

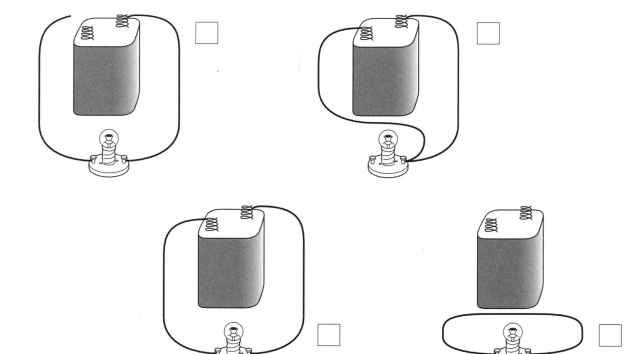

Primary Science Kit: Pupil Resource Book Years 1–2 © Rosemary Sherrington, Nelson Thornes Ltd, 2002